MW01492521

LOST &
FOUND

A Prodigal's Journey

LOST & FOUND

A Prodigal's Journey

ROBERT MORRIS

STUDY GUIDE

Lost and Found Study Guide
Copyright © 2018 by Robert Morris

Content taken from sermons delivered in 2015 by Robert Morris at Gateway Church, Southlake, TX.

Unless otherwise noted, all Scripture quotations are taken from the New King James Version®. Copyright © 1982 by Thomas Nelson. Used by permission. All rights reserved.

Scripture quotations marked (KJV) are taken from the King James Version of the Bible. Public domain.

Scripture quotations marked MSG are taken from *THE MESSAGE*, copyright © 1993, 1994, 1995, 1996, 2000, 2001, 2002 by Eugene H. Peterson. Used by permission of NavPress. All rights reserved. Represented by Tyndale House Publishers, Inc.

Scripture quotations taken from the New American Standard Bible® (NASB), copyright © 1960, 1962, 1963, 1968, 1971, 1972, 1973, 1975, 1977, 1995 by The Lockman Foundation. Used by permission. www.Lockman.org.

Scripture quotations marked (NLT) are taken from the Holy Bible, New Living Translation, copyright © 1996, 2004, 2015 by Tyndale House Foundation. Used by permission of Tyndale House Publishers, Inc., Carol Stream, Illinois 60188. All rights reserved.

All rights reserved. No portion of this publication may be reproduced, stored in a retrieval system, or transmitted in any form by any means—electronic, mechanical, photocopying, recording, or any other—without prior permission from the publisher. "Gateway Press" and Gateway Publishing" are trademarks registered in the United States Patent and Trademark Office by Gateway Church.

ISBN: 978-1-945529-85-6
eBook ISBN: 978-1-949399-75-2

We hope you hear from the Holy Spirit and receive God's richest blessings from this book by Gateway Press. We want to provide the highest quality resources that take the messages, music, and media of Gateway Church to the world. For more information on other resources from Gateway Publishing®, go to gatewaypublishing.com.

Gateway Press, an imprint of Gateway Publishing
700 Blessed Way
Southlake, Texas 76092
gatewaypublishing.com

Printed in the United States of America
18 19 20 21 22   7 6 5 4 3 2 1

CONTENTS

1

THE BELIEVER'S BATTLE

Every believer experiences a battle between their spirit, which is already saved, and their soul, which is being saved.

ENGAGE

Describe a time when you got lost (e.g., as a child in a store or as an adult in a new city).

WATCH

Watch "The Believer's Battle."

- Look for the difference between the finished work of grace in your spirit and the progressive work of grace in your soul.
- Think about what it means to follow Jesus and pick up your cross *daily*.

(If you are not able to watch this teaching on video, read the following. Otherwise, skip to the **Talk** section after viewing.)

READ

The story of the prodigal son is one of the most well-known parables in the Bible.

> "A certain man had two sons. And the younger of them said to *his* father, 'Father, give me the portion of goods that falls *to me.*' So he divided to them *his* livelihood. And not many days after, the younger son gathered all together, journeyed to a far country, and there wasted his possessions with prodigal living" (Luke 15:11–13).

The Greek word translated *prodigal* means "dissolutely." A dissolute person, according to Webster's dictionary, is "lacking in restraint; marked by indulgence in things (such as drink or promiscuous sex)."[1] If we're being honest, there is probably at least one area (if not more) in our lives in which we lack restraint, even if just for a short time. In that area we tend to be prodigal.

Why do we have such prodigal tendencies? We are made up of three parts: spirit, soul, and body. All three parts are mentioned in Genesis 2:7:

> The Lord God formed man of the **dust** of the ground; and breathed into his nostrils the **breath of life**; and man became a living **soul** (KJV, emphasis added).

---

[1]Merriam-Webster Dictionary online, accessed 4/10/18, https://www.merriam -webster.com/dictionary/dissolute.

The "breath of life" refers to your spirit, which God created to relate to Himself. "Dust" refers to your body, which God created to relate to His creation. The "soul" includes your mind, will, and emotions, and God created it to relate both to Him *and* to His creation.

God did not design humans to relate to Him with just their souls. However, when Adam and Eve sinned, their spirits died, and people have been born with dead spirits ever since. Your spirit comes alive when you accept Christ, but until then, you relate to God only through your soul. You relate to Him through what you understand, how you feel about situations, and what you desire to do. In other words, you make all your decisions based on your thoughts, feelings, and desires. Your soul likes being in charge, even though God never intended it to be that way.

Here are some important things we need to understand about the soul:

The Soul Is Selfish

The soul's motto is "protect number one" (yourself). It tells you to do what you think, reason, or feel is "right" for you. The mind is part of the soul, and it records everything you have ever heard, seen, or experienced. This information is stored in your subconscious. In a millisecond, your mind can assess a situation and ask, "Have I ever seen, heard, or experienced anything like this before?" Then it will compare that situation with all the other past experiences in your subconscious. This is why you can be in a conversation and suddenly get very angry but not know why. It's because your subconscious remembers a previous conversation that didn't go so well, and it tells your mind, "Be more forceful this time!" The same process is true for situations in which you suddenly feel insecure or afraid. Your spirit may say, "Lay your life down and turn the other cheek," but your soul says, "Protect number one."

This is also why you can immediately dislike a person after just meeting them. Your mind asks, "Have I ever met anyone like this before?" and your subconscious answers, "Yes, you've met four people almost exactly like this person, and one of them pulled your shorts down in Physical Education in seventh grade." You may have only known a person for a few minutes, but your mind says, *I know exactly what kind of person you are!*

A stronghold works the same way. Take lust, for example. Your mind has categorized every perverse thing you have ever seen. Therefore, when you see something that reminds you of one of those things, you begin to have lustful thoughts. This is why believers fall away and find themselves in spiritual pigpens—they have stronghold in their souls.

If you've accepted Christ, your spirit *is* saved. Many people have a problem understanding grace and works, though. They don't understand the finished work of grace in the spirit and the progressive work of grace in the soul. Some people on the "grace" side preach unrighteous living, but grace was never intended to be used as an excuse. Then there are those on the "works" side who preach legalism, but that only puts people in more bondage. We must understand that even though our spirits are saved, there is still a real, on-going battle in our souls.

Your soul is born selfish. That is why it needs to be converted (see Psalm 19:7), renewed, and transformed. Verses such as Hebrews 10:39 and James 1:21 speak of "the saving of the soul," but this is separate from eternal salvation. The Greek word for saving is *sozo,* which means 'making whole.' If you're a believer, your spirit has already been made whole. But your soul still needs to be saved. So how does this happen?

The Soul Must Submit to the Spirit

Romans 9:12, referring to Jacob and Esau, says, "The older shall serve the younger." This is a principle God uses throughout Scripture. Imagine you live for 20 years before you accept Christ. Who's in charge for those 20 years? Your soul is. Then you get born again, and your spirit comes alive. It says to your soul, "I'm in charge now. We're going to do things God's way." Does your soul, being the sweet, kind, compassionate, humble person that it is, say, "Okay"? No! Your soul says, "Not without a fight!" That's where the battle begins. Are you going to respond the way your soul—your mind, will, and emotions—tells you to, or are you going to respond as Jesus would in that situation?

You have to feed your spirit so that it grows up and gets stronger. Many of us spend more time feeding our souls garbage on the internet than feeding our spirits the Word of God. David talks about the battle of the soul in Psalm 131:2:

> Surely I have calmed and quieted my soul,
> Like a weaned child with his mother;
> Like a weaned child *is* my soul within me.

A mother weans her child by giving him solid food instead of milk. Your soul needs to be weaned too. The apostle Paul wrote to the believers in Corinth, "I, brethren, could not speak to you as to spiritual *people* but as to carnal, as to babes in Christ. I fed you with milk and not with solid food" (1 Corinthians 3:1–2). And here is what the writer of Hebrews says:

> For though by this time you ought to be teachers, you need *someone* to teach you again the first principles of the oracles of God; and you have come to need milk and not solid food. For everyone who partakes *only* of milk *is* unskilled in the word of righteousness, for he is a babe. But solid food belongs to those who are of full age, *that is,* those who by reason of use have their senses exercised to discern both good and evil (Hebrews 5:12–14).

What happens when you try to wean a baby? He throws a fit and cries. He thinks you're trying to kill him by taking away the only food source he's ever known. Your soul has the same reaction to being weaned. It throws a fit and cries because it thinks you are trying to kill it. In this case, though, you really are!

The Soul Must Die

Your selfish thoughts need to die. This idea of dying to self is found throughout Christian theology:

> For the word of God *is* living and powerful, and sharper than any two-edged sword, piercing even to the division of soul and spirit, and of joints and marrow, and is a discerner of the thoughts and intents of the heart. And there is no creature hidden from His sight, but all things *are* naked and open to the eyes of Him to whom we *must give* account (Hebrews 4:12–13).

"The division of soul and spirit" is what you think versus what God thinks. The word "open" in verse 13 is the Greek word *trachelizo*. It means 'to bend back the neck of a victim to be slain; to expose the gullet of a person to kill him.' Let me tell you: God has big plans for your soul! When believers go astray, it's because they don't have the sword (God's Word) to divide between their soul and spirit.

Jesus gave His disciples these instructions:

> "If anyone desires to come after Me, let him deny himself, and take up his cross, and follow Me. For whoever desires to save his life will lose it, but whoever loses his life for My sake will find it" (Matthew 16:24–25).

The word for "life" in this verse is the Greek word *psuche*, which means 'soul.' Have you ever heard the saying, "Jesus went to the cross so you wouldn't have to"? I have a problem with that quote because this passage says I have to die too. I have to pick up my cross and follow Jesus.

In Luke 9:23, Jesus takes it a step further: "If anyone desires to come after Me, let him deny himself, and take up his cross daily, and follow Me." And in 1 Corinthians 15:31, Paul says, "I die daily." *Daily*! Paul isn't saying he gets saved every day; rather, he crucifies his soul every day. A person may say, "I just want to walk down the aisle one time." It doesn't work that way, though. You need to come to the cross *every* day.

In Romans 12:1–2, Paul instructs us to "present your bodies a living sacrifice, holy, acceptable to God, *which is* your reasonable service. And do not be conformed to this world, but be transformed by the renewing of your mind." Why would believers ever leave the family of God and live in a pigpen as the prodigal son did? Because they are not renewing their minds. They are not feeding their spirits with God's Word every day.

When I was on sabbatical, the Lord convicted me that I had developed a bad habit of having "drive-through" quiet times. He said, "You used to spend a lot more time with Me." I repented and began setting aside more time for the Lord. Then He reminded me that when I was 30 years old, He taught me how to have a quiet time. Back then, I was beginning to have headaches, and doctors could not figure out why. The Lord knew why, though. He told me the reason I was having headaches was because I wasn't really spending time with Him. He said, "Stress and sin snowball." As the Lord brought this memory to my mind, I felt as if He directed me to read Psalm 32 in *The Message*. Verse 6 says, "These things add up. Every one of us needs to pray" (MSG).

I don't want to be a prodigal, and I don't want you to be a prodigal either. This is the battle every believer faces: are we going to let the Word of God divide between our thoughts and God's thoughts? Or are we going to keep allowing our souls to control us?

NOTES

_____

_____

_____

_____

_____

_____

_____

_____

_____

_____

_____

_____

_____

TALK

These questions can be used for group discussion or personal reflection.

Question 1

Read Luke 15:11–13. What are some areas of your life in which you struggle (or have struggled) with restraint?

_____

_____

_____

_____

Question 2

How has sin changed the way people relate to God?

_____

_____

_____

_____

Question 3
Read Hebrews 10:39 and James 1:21. What is the difference between the finished work of grace in your spirit and the progressive work of grace in your soul?

_____

_____

_____

_____

Question 4
Why is feeding your spirit with the Word of God essential to winning the battle with your soul?

_____

_____

_____

_____

PRAY

If studying alone, ask the Holy Spirit to reveal the truth about Himself to you. If in a group, take some time to pray for each other as you think about the truths discussed in this session.

EXPLORE

Do you want to go deeper with this teaching? Here are some additional things to think about, pray for, or write about in your journal throughout the next week.

Key Thought

> *When you accept Christ, your spirit comes alive and says, "I'm in charge now. We're going to do things God's way." But your soul says, "Not without a fight!" That's where the battle begins.*

What is the difference between responding to situations according the desires of your soul and responding as Jesus would?

_____

_____

_____

_____

Key Verses
Luke 15:11–13; Genesis 2:7; Psalm 131:2; Hebrews 4:12–13; 5:12–14
What truths stand out to you as you read these verses?

_____

_____

What is the Holy Spirit saying to you through these Scriptures?

_____

_____

Key Question
Read Luke 9:23 and 1 Corinthians 15:21. What would it look like for you to "die daily"?

Key Prayer
Lord, thank You for the miracle of salvation. I am so grateful that my eternity is secure in You. Please help me recognize the battle between my spirit and my soul and guide me as I strengthen my spirit through Your Word. I submit all my thoughts, feelings, and desires to You. May every part of my life bring You glory and honor. In Jesus' name, Amen.

2

THE WAY HOME

The key to coming home is honesty. We must learn to be honest with ourselves, with others, and with God.

RECAP

In the previous session, we learned there is a battle between our souls (our mind, will, and emotions) and our spirits. Our spirits are immediately saved when we accept Christ, but our souls begin a life-long process of being transformed. We must feed our spirits with God's Word and renew our minds every day if we are going to win the battle.

Did you recognize any areas of your life in which you need to die to self this past week?

ENGAGE

What's the best advice you've ever received?

WATCH

Watch "The Way Home."
- Look for the definition of integrity.
- Think about the people in your life with whom you need to be honest.

(If you are not able to watch this teaching on video, read the following. Otherwise, skip to the **Talk** section after viewing.)

READ

All of us are prodigal at some time in some area of our lives—perhaps even right now. But if you've been away from God, how do you come home? We find the answer in the story of the prodigal son:

> "But when he **came to himself**, he said, 'How many of my father's hired servants have bread enough and to spare, and I perish with hunger! I will arise and go to my father, and will say to him, "**Father**, I have sinned against heaven and before you, and I am no longer worthy to be called your son. Make me like one of your hired **servants**"'" (Luke 15:17–19, emphasis added).

The way home can be summed up in one word: *honesty.* "He came to himself" means the prodigal son was willing to honest with himself. He was also willing to be honest with others. After all, the other servants would know he was the son who squandered his inheritance. Finally, the prodigal son was willing to be honest with his father. If you are a believer, you have a heavenly Father. To come home, you must be willing to be honest with yourself, others, and Him.

Be Honest with Yourself

The way home starts with being honest with yourself.

> Abraham journeyed from there to the South, and dwelt between Kadesh and Shur, and stayed in Gerar. Now Abraham said of Sarah

his wife, "She *is* my sister." And Abimelech king of Gerar sent and took Sarah.

But God came to Abimelech in a dream by night, and said to him, "Indeed you *are* a dead man because of the woman whom you have taken, for she *is* a man's wife."

But Abimelech had not come near her; and he said, "Lord, will You slay a righteous nation also? Did he not say to me, 'She *is* my sister'? And she, even she herself said, 'He *is* my brother.' In the integrity of my heart and innocence of my hands I have done this."

And God said to him in a dream, "Yes, I know that you did this in the integrity of your heart. For I also withheld you from sinning against Me; therefore I did not let you touch her" (Genesis 20:1-6).

This is an amazing story. Because Abimelech was walking in the "integrity of his heart," God kept him from sinning. The Hebrew word for *integrity* in this passage means 'completeness.' It refers to selling something and not holding anything back. If you hold something back, then you aren't dealing with integrity. This is the reason that when testifying, you promise to tell the truth, the *whole truth*, and nothing but the truth. If you don't tell the whole truth, then you're not being honest.

Be Honest with Others

The prodigal son said, "Make me like one of your hired servants" (Luke 15:19). He knew the other servants would know who he was and ask him lots of questions. He would have to explain how he left home and squandered everything. Even though it would be humiliating, the prodigal son was willing to humble himself in front of other people and be honest.

Have you ever heard someone say, "I'm going to be honest with you now"? Don't you want to reply, "What have you been until now?" James 5:16 says, "Confess *your* trespasses to one another, and pray for one another, that you may be healed." The Greek word for trespasses here is *paraptoma. Paraptoma* has two definitions. One is 'a lapse or deviation from truth and uprightness.' As believers, we need to confession our "deviations from truth" to others to be healed. The second definition is 'to fall beside or near something.' The prefix *para* means 'beside or alongside.' For example, the word *parable* come from *para* and *bole*, which means 'to throw.' A parable is a story Jesus would "throw" right beside the truth. Another word you may know is *Parakletos*, which refers to the Person who walks beside us—the Holy Spirit. God wants to walk right beside you!

Notice that when you fall right beside the truth—just barely miss it—you must confess it. If you won't confess the little things, you definitely won't confess the big things. When you get in the habit of bringing the little things into the light, you'll understand that you can bring the big things as well.

It reminds me of the Greek word *hamartano*, which means 'to miss the mark.' Most of the time, this word is translated as *sin*. If you miss the mark by a mile or by an inch, you ought to bring it into the light. Why? Because Satan only works in darkness; he can't work in the light.

I want to ask you something that may hit close to home: can you confess to your spouse if you're struggling with lust? Can your spouse confess to you if he or she is struggling with lust? Ladies, if he won't tell you, whom is he going to tell? If he can't tell you without you blowing up or getting insecure or fearful, he'll learn to keep it in the dark. He'll be trained to keep it secret.

I can share my struggles with my wife, Debbie. When I was 25 years old, I came clean with her about my struggles with lust, and God began to do a cleansing work in my life. By God's grace, Debbie understood that I love her, and my struggles in an area don't mean otherwise.

I want to give you an illustration, and I'm going to use food addiction as the example. Now, I know food addiction and lust have very different consequences, but both struggles are appetites of the flesh. Suppose I had an addiction to sugar, and after work one day, I confessed to my wife, "I ate a dozen Krispy Kreme donuts on the way home." Confessing that fault to my wife wouldn't make her doubt my love for her. Instead, Debbie would know that I have an appetite that needs to be solved in a godly way.

Before I was saved, I developed an appetite for lust. I've now walked in victory for many years, but one of the reasons for this victory is that I talk to Debbie. Ladies, it would be better for your husband to struggle with you than for him to struggle with another woman.

This isn't just for married people, either. Single people need to have someone with whom they can talk. If you're dating or engaged, it's important *not* to give your significant other what the world says you have to give them to keep them. If you do, they could develop an unhealthy appetite that they will try to satisfy later. Please hear me on this, though. If you have experienced infidelity in your marriage, it's not your fault. Nothing excuses adultery.

When I came clean to Debbie, I told her every bad thing I'd ever done. Her response was, "I knew you were bad when I married you. I didn't know you were *that* bad, but I knew you were bad." She thanked me for telling her, and then she reminded me why she married me: "I knew you loved God and I knew you loved me even though you had struggles. And I love you."

Be Honest with God

The son was going home to be completely honest with his father. He wasn't going to hold anything back.

In Acts 5, we read about a couple who did hold something back:

> A certain man named Ananias, with Sapphira his wife, sold a possession. And he kept back *part* of the proceeds, his wife also being aware *of it,* and brought a certain part and laid *it* at the apostles' feet. But Peter said, "Ananias, why has Satan filled your heart to lie to the Holy Spirit and keep back *part* of the price of the land for yourself?" (Acts 5:1-3).

Ananias acted as if he brought all of the proceeds to the apostles, but he actually kept some for himself. He lied to Peter (a person), but the apostle asked. "Why has Satan filled your heart to lie to the Holy Spirit?" When you lie to yourself and to others, you are lying to God. Another way to say this is if you aren't walking in honesty with yourself and others, you aren't walking in honesty with God either.

Have you ever walked into a room and seen a child try to hide something behind his back? When you asked the child what was in his hand, he probably said, "Nothing." But were you fooled? Of course not. Now picture yourself as that child. Do you think God is ever fooled by you? Don't you think He can see whatever you're trying to hide? God can see exactly what you have in your hand. And here's the good news—Jesus already died for whatever it is.

The best example of being honest with God is a prayer by Jesus Himself in the Garden of Gethsemane. It is one of the most amazing passages in the Bible.

> He was withdrawn from them about a stone's throw, and He knelt down and prayed, saying, "Father, if it is Your will, take this cup away from Me; nevertheless not My will, but Yours, be done" (Luke 22:41–42).

Matthew 26:39–44 tells us that Jesus prayed this prayer three times: "Not my will, but Yours, be done." That prayer was as honest as you could be. In my opinion, Jesus wasn't talking about the nails and the thorns and the scourging. He was talking about being separated from God, which was necessary for humanity to be redeemed.

Jesus was being honest. The word *will* means desire. Jesus was saying, "This is My desire. If there's any other way, please show Me now."

You will never truthfully pray, "Your will be done" until you truthfully pray, "Not my will." And you will never truthfully pray, "Not my will" until you admit what your desire really is. That's what Jesus was doing.

NOTES

_____

_____

_____

_____

_____

_____

_____

_____

_____

_____

_____

_____

TALK

These questions can be used for group discussion or personal reflection.

Question 1

How does Scripture define *integrity?* How does this definition contrast with the world's view of "honesty"?

_____

_____

_____

_____

Question 2

Read Genesis 20:1-6. Why does the way home begin with being honest with yourself?

_____

_____

_____

_____

Question 3
Read Acts 5:1–3. Why do you think integrity is so important to God?

_____

_____

_____

_____

Question 4
How would praying "Not my will, but Yours, be done" and really meaning it change your life?

_____

_____

_____

_____

PRAY

If studying alone, ask the Holy Spirit to reveal the truth about Himself to you. If in a group, take some time to pray for each other as you think about the truths discussed in this session.

EXPLORE

Do you want to go deeper with this teaching? Here are some additional things to think about, pray for, or write about in your journal throughout the next week:

Key Thought

If you won't confess the little things, you definitely won't confess the big things. When you get in the habit of bringing the little things into the light, you'll understand that you can bring the big things as well.

It takes courage to begin confessing the little things. Write down the names of some trustworthy people with whom you can share your struggles.

_____ _____

_____

_____

_____ _____

Key Verses

Luke 15:17-19; Genesis 20:1-6; James 5:16; Luke 22:41-42

What truths stand out to you as you read these verses?

_____

_____

What is the Holy Spirit saying to you through these Scriptures?

_____

_____

Key Question

How would your life be different if you were completely honest with yourself, others, and God?

Key Prayer

Heavenly Father, thank You for loving me so much that You sent Jesus to save me. I love You, and I want to walk with integrity in my heart. Holy Spirit, please convict me of any area of my life that isn't pleasing to you. Help me bring my struggles into the light and be honest with myself, others, and especially You. I want Your will, not mine, to be done. In Jesus' name, Amen.

3

THE BROTHER'S BATTLE

No one is righteous enough to earn salvation. It comes only by grace through faith in Jesus' work on the cross.

RECAP

In the previous session, we learned the key to coming home is honesty. Honesty means telling the *whole* truth and holding nothing back. We must learn to bring both little and big things into the light and be honest with ourselves, others, and God.

Did you find it easier to be honest about your struggles this past week?

ENGAGE

If you could meet any famous person, who would it be and why?

WATCH

Watch "The Brother's Battle."

- Look for the attitude of the Scribes and Pharisees.
- Consider how pride can be a problem for all of us.

(If you are not able to watch this teaching on video, read the following. Otherwise, skip to the **Talk** section after viewing.)

READ

The story of the prodigal son features two sons: the younger one, who squandered his inheritance on prodigal living, and the older one, who stayed home. How do you think the older son felt when his prodigal brother came home and received a party? And how do you feel toward people who struggle with sin in their lives?

> "Now his older son was in the field. And as he came and drew near to the house, he heard music and dancing. So he called one of the servants and asked what these things meant. And he said to him, 'Your brother has come, and because he has received him safe and sound, your father has killed the fatted calf.'
>
> But he was angry and would not go in. Therefore his father came out and pleaded with him. So he answered and said to *his* father, 'Lo, these many years I have been serving you; I **never** transgressed your commandment at any time; and yet you **never** gave me a young goat, that I might make merry with my friends" (Luke 15:25-29 emphasis added).

What is the brother's battle? It's keeping your heart right when the Father rejoices over sinners coming home. It's not allowing jealousy, envy, anger, or bitterness to come in—even when the prodigal is gone and hasn't come back yet. Think about the father standing on the front porch every night and looking for his younger son. The older son watches his father and begins to believe the lie of the enemy that the father is mistreating him by loving the prodigal son even more.

There are three parables in Luke 15: the lost sheep, the lost coin, and the lost son. The reason Jesus told these parables is because the Pharisees were upset that He was receiving sinners (see Luke 15:1-3).

The brother's battle does three things:

It Affects How We See Ourselves

In verse 29, the older brother says he *never* transgressed his father's commandment at any time. That's a lie, though. He was human. Romans 3:23 says, "All have sinned and fall short of the glory of God." The apostle Paul also writes, "There is none righteous, no, not one" (Romans 3:10). The only Son who never sinned at any time is Jesus. But that's the way the brother saw himself.

In Luke 18:9-14, Jesus tells another parable to "some who trusted in themselves that they were righteous, and despised others":

> "Two men went up to the temple to pray, one a Pharisee and the other a tax collector. The Pharisee stood and prayed thus with himself, 'God, I thank You that I am not like other men—extortioners, unjust, adulterers, or even as this tax collector. I fast twice a week; I give tithes of all that I possess.' And the tax collector, standing afar off, would not so much as raise *his* eyes to heaven, but beat his breast, saying, 'God, be merciful to me a sinner!' I tell you, this man went down to his house justified *rather* than the other; for everyone who exalts himself will be humbled, and he who humbles himself will be exalted."

I think many mature believers have, at one time or another, felt the same way as the Pharisee—proud of their own "holiness." Yet the tax collector was the one who was justified. The battle is trusting your own righteousness. No new believer has this battle. This pride develops over time and can manifest many years later. The devil is happy when we think that our good works make us right with God and better than others.

We battle with low self-esteem and high self-esteem. But take out the low, high, and esteem, and you see that what we battle with is "self." The focus shouldn't be on yourself, though; it should be on Christ. Whether you have a good week or a bad week, you can still praise God.

It Affects How We See Others

"Then one of the Pharisees asked Him to eat with him. And He went to the Pharisee's house, and sat down to eat. And behold, a woman in the city who was a sinner, when she knew that *Jesus* sat at the table in the Pharisee's house, brought an alabaster flask of fragrant oil, and stood at His feet behind *Him* weeping; and she began to wash His feet with her tears, and wiped *them* with the hair of her head; and she kissed His feet and anointed *them* with the fragrant oil. Now when the Pharisee who had invited Him saw *this,* he spoke to himself, saying, "This Man, if He were a prophet, would know who and what manner of woman *this is* who is touching Him, for she is a sinner."

And Jesus answered and said to him, "Simon, I have something to say to you."

So he said, "Teacher, say it."

"There was a certain creditor who had two debtors. One owed five hundred denarii, and the other fifty. And when they had nothing with which to repay, he freely forgave them both. Tell Me, therefore, which of them will love him more?"

Simon answered and said, "I suppose the *one* whom he forgave more."

And He said to him, "You have rightly judged." Then He turned to the woman and said to Simon, "Do you see this woman? I entered your house; you gave Me no water for My feet, but she has washed My feet with her tears and wiped *them* with the hair of her head. You gave Me no kiss, but this woman has not ceased to kiss My feet since the time I came in. You did not anoint My head with oil, but this woman has anointed My feet with fragrant oil. Therefore I say to you, her sins, which *are* many, are forgiven, for she loved much. But to whom little is forgiven, *the same* loves little" (Luke 7:36–47).

Notice the Pharisee "spoke to himself." He was thinking, and Jesus answered his thoughts. This parable does not teach that some people are better (or worse) than others; instead, it teaches that there are some people who *think* they are better (or worse) than others. Jesus uses amounts because He's answering Simon's thoughts. According to Scripture, however, if you've broken one commandment, you've broken them all. We all owe the same. Jesus paid the same price for all of us, no matter how much we may have sinned.

If you look up to *you*, then you will look down on others. That was the problem with the Pharisee and with the older brother.

It Affects How We See the Father

The emphasis of Jesus' parables in Luke 15 is on the idea that someone lost something precious. The shepherd lost a sheep. The woman lost a coin. And a father lost a son. The whole reason Jesus told these three parables is to show us how much God the Father grieves when He loses something precious—His children.

The older son didn't get it. He said the father had never given him a goat, yet the father gave *both* sons their inheritance. The inheritance of the firstborn was double the amount of any other children. The older brother got twice as much, but because he never saw himself correctly and never saw others correctly, he didn't see his father correctly either. The father said the older son had his presence and his provision (see v. 31). The younger missed out on it because he left home physically, but the older son missed out on it because he left home in his heart. He allowed insecurity, anger, fear, and jealousy to build up in his heart toward his brother and father.

So how do you win the brother's battle? You win it the way the apostle Paul did:

- AD 56: Ten years before his death and twenty years into his ministry, he calls himself the "least of the apostles" (1 Corinthians 15:9).
- AD 63: Three years before his death, he calls himself "the very least of all saints" (Ephesians 3:8 NASB).

- AD 65: One year before his death, he calls himself the "chief" of sinners (1 Timothy 1:15).

Why did Paul write about dying daily and being crucified with Christ? Because he focused on the cross: "For I decided that while I was with you I would forget everything except Jesus Christ, the one who was crucified" (1 Corinthians 2:2 NLT).

The only way you are going to win the brother's battle is to stay close to the cross—to remember that it is Jesus' sacrifice that saved us all.

NOTES

_____

_____

_____

_____

_____

_____

_____

_____

_____

_____

TALK

These questions can be used for group discussion or personal reflection.

Question 1

Why did Jesus tell the parables in Luke 15? What is the emphasis of these three stories?

_____

_____

_____

_____

Question 2

What is the common link between low self-esteem and high self-esteem?

_____

_____

_____

_____

Question 3
Why do you think mature believers struggle with the brother's battle?

_____

_____

_____

_____

Question 4
Why did the prodigal son miss out on his father's presence and provision? Why did the older brother miss out on the same things?

_____

_____

_____

_____

Question 5
Read 1 Corinthians 15:9, Ephesians 3:8, and 1 Timothy 1:15. How does the apostle Paul describe himself?

_____

_____

_____

_____

PRAY

If studying alone, ask the Holy Spirit to reveal the truth about Himself to you. If in a group, take some time to pray for each other as you think about the truths discussed in this session.

EXPLORE

Do you want to go deeper with this teaching? Here are some additional things to think about, pray for, or write about in your journal throughout the next week:

Key Thought

> *We all owe the same. It cost the blood of Jesus for all of us. If Simon understood that he owed Jesus as much as the woman did, then he would have loved Jesus as much as the woman did.*

Does your love for God depend on how "bad" or "good" you were before you accepted Christ? Why or why not?

_____

_____

_____

_____

Key Verses

Luke 15:1-3, 25-29; 18:9-14; Romans 3:10, 23; Luke 7:36-47

What truths stand out to you as you read these verses?

_____

_____

What is the Holy Spirit saying to you through these Scriptures?

_____

_____

Key Question

Even though we remember him as the apostle who wrote much of the New Testament, Paul refers to himself as the "chief" of sinners. Why is this perspective crucial for winning the brother's battle?

Key Prayer

Lord, thank You for saving me. I recognize that salvation is an incredible gift, one I could never earn for myself. Holy Spirit, please convict me any time I begin to trust in my own righteousness or think of myself as better than others. Show me anything in my heart that isn't pleasing to You. Please help me keep my focus off myself and on the cross. In Jesus' name, Amen.

4

THE TRUMP CARD BATTLE

Satan wants to use secrets, sin, and shame as trump cards in your life.
The only way to defeat him is to bring everything to the cross.

RECAP

In the previous session, we learned the brother's battle affects how we see ourselves, others, and God. We must remember that everyone is a sinner, and salvation is *only* by grace through faith—never by our works. The way to win the brother's battle is to keep our focus off ourselves and on the cross.

Did you find any new ways to keep your focus on the cross this past week?

ENGAGE

What was your favorite game to play as a child? What is your favorite game to play as an adult?

WATCH

Watch "The Trump Card Battle."

- Watch for the ways Satan can gain an advantage over you.
- Consider what your mind is focused on and if there are any areas of weakness Satan can exploit.

(If you are not able to watch this teaching on video, read the following. Otherwise, skip to the **Talk** section after viewing.)

READ

In many games of cards, like Spades and Bridge, there is a suit (such as Hearts or Diamonds) that is trumps. This means you can play a high card of another suit, and even the lowest card of the trump suit will beat your high card. If we are not careful as believers, we give Satan a trump card in our lives. We may be going to church, tithing, and participating in groups—all "high cards" in Christian life. But if there is one area of our lives that isn't surrendered to the Lord, Satan can use it as a trump card. Suddenly, we find ourselves out of the game.

Sometimes we even tell Satan what a trump card for us would be. We say things like, "I couldn't trust God anymore if this happened" or "If my spouse did this, it would be the end of our marriage." When you make statement such as those, the enemy knows the exact areas in which to work against you. Don't give him any trump cards.

The story of the prodigal son shows us three areas of life that can be trump cards:

Secrets

Luke 15:13 says, "Not many days after, the younger son gathered all together, journeyed to a far country, and there wasted his possessions with prodigal living." The phrase "not many days after" tells us the prodigal son had been planning his actions. He had it in his heart and mind before he got the inheritance, and that's why he asked for it. He had a secret: he thought he would be happy if he had money.

Secrets are thoughts with which we allow the enemy to build a case in our minds. Second Corinthians 10:5 speaks of "casting down imaginations (KJV)." The root of the word "imaginations" is *image. Image* comes from a Latin word that means 'I make.' The root actually means 'I become.' **What you picture in your mind is what you become**. Don't have a picture in your mind of something that is ungodly. Don't imagine a good marriage with someone other than your spouse. Imagine a good marriage with your spouse! Don't imagine being rich one day. Imagine being generous now! The prodigal son had the wrong thought in his mind, and as soon as he received his inheritance, he fulfilled his secret.

Read these opening words of the Bible:

> In the beginning God created the heavens and the earth. The earth was without form, and void; and darkness *was* on the face of the deep. And the Spirit of God was hovering over the face of the waters.
>
> Then God said, "Let there be light"; and there was light. And God saw the light, that *it was* good; and God divided the light from the darkness (Genesis 1:1–4).

Notice God didn't create the darkness. It was already there. Many theologians believe this was because Satan had already been cast out of heaven and fallen to the earth. God never said, "Let there be darkness," and He never said the darkness was good.

> And I remind you of the angels who did not stay within the limits
> of authority God gave them but left the place where they belonged.
> God has kept them securely chained in prisons of darkness, waiting
> for the great day of judgment (Jude 6 NLT).

There are fallen angels (demonic spirits), and they live in darkness
just like Satan. Secrets live in darkness too. The best thing you can
do with a secret is to bring it into the light.

Sin

Sin is the second trump card. *Prodigal* means "without restraint,"
and the prodigal son's sins were already in his heart.

> Now Jacob cooked a stew, and Esau came in from the field, and he
> *was* weary. And Esau said to Jacob, "Please feed me with that same
> red *stew*, for I *am* weary." Therefore his name was called Edom.
> But Jacob said, "Sell me your birthright as of this day."
> And Esau said, "Look, I *am* about to die; so what *is* this
> birthright to me?"
> Then Jacob said, "Swear to me as of this day."
> So he swore to him, and sold his birthright to Jacob. And Jacob
> gave Esau bread and stew of lentils; then he ate and drank, arose, and
> went his way. Thus Esau despised *his* birthright (Genesis 25:29–34).

The New Testament tells us not to be like Esau, who sold his
birthright for a morsel of food. The birthright was phenomenal

in the Jewish culture. The firstborn was honored and valued. He received twice as much inheritance as any other child in the family. He could also borrow money simply on his name, and he was automatically made an elder at the gates of the city. Esau gave all this up for a bowl of stew. The New Testament likens this to sexual sin. It is like any fleshly appetite. I know people who have given up *everything* for one short moment of gratification. They've given up their marriage, family, business, and the call of God on their lives for one fleshly appetite.

Romans 8:29 says Jesus was "the firstborn among many brethren." He made each of us the firstborn of God also. We have all the rights and privileges of the firstborn of the Father who created everything. Sin causes us to give all that up. **Sin always takes you farther than you wanted to go, costs you more than you wanted to pay, and requires more than you wanted to give**. It always does. That's the way sin is.

It is difficult for many believers to understand the Old Testament passages in which God says to kill an entire nation—even the children. However, God had given these nations the chance to repent. They refused to accept Him and continued in their false worship. God told Saul to kill *all* the Amalekites, but he didn't do it. Saul ended up fighting the Amalekites his entire life, and he died in an Amalekite battle. Saul didn't kill the children, so they grew up and killed him instead.

You need to kill your sins while they are still small, or else they will grow up and kill you.

Shame

Shame is the result of the fall. It was the first thing Adam and Eve felt after they sinned. God had never given His children any reason to be afraid, so He must have grieved the day they hid from Him.

How do you think the prodigal son felt after the party? What about the rest of his life? He was still ashamed of what he did. People surely talked about him. His relationship with his father was restored, but he lost some things forever. His inheritance was gone. He couldn't go back to the bar owners and prostitutes and get his money back. Like the prodigal son, we can be forgiven and healed, and we can have full, joyful lives. However, we may still have to deal with things that God never intended.

There are two types of people who feel shame: those who deal with pride and those who deal with insecurity. Here's another way to identify these people: they either talk too much or not much at all. The prideful person talks too much to cover up who he really is. The insecure person doesn't say much because he doesn't want you to see his shame.

Satan knows you still carry shame, and as soon as you try to do something for God, he'll try to bring your past out as a trump card against you. So what's the answer?

> Therefore we also, since we are surrounded by so great a cloud of witnesses, let us lay aside every weight, and the sin which so easily ensnares *us,* and let us run with endurance the race that is

set before us, looking unto Jesus, the author and finisher of *our* faith, who for the joy that was set before Him endured the cross, despising the shame, and has sat down at the right hand of the throne of God (Hebrews 12:1-2).

Jesus is the author *and* finisher of our faith. That's great news! First Corinthians 1:18 says, "For the message of the cross is foolishness to those who are perishing, but to us who are being saved it is the power of God."

How do you get rid of your trump cards? Go to the cross. You don't just go to the cross one time to get saved. Yes, salvation is a new beginning and a spiritual birth, but the cross is the power of God. We need to take our secrets, sin, and shame to the cross every day.

Remember, God has already played the *highest* trump card. Satan may hold the two of Spades, but God holds the Ace of Spades. Satan can lay out all the cards and say, "Look at all you've done wrong." But God says, "Look at all My Son did right." Because of the cross of Jesus Christ, you are forgiven and free.

NOTES

_____ _____

_____ _____

_____ _____

_____ _____

_____ _____

TALK

These questions can be used for group discussion or personal reflection.

Question 1
What are the three common trump cards the enemy tries to use against believers?

_____

_____

_____

_____

Question 2
Why do secrets live in darkness? Are there any secrets you need to bring into the light?

_____

_____

_____

_____

Question 3

Read Genesis 25:29–34 and Romans 8:29. What does it mean to you to be a "firstborn" child of God?

_____

_____

_____

_____

Question 4

Why is it important to deal with "little" sins before they grow?

_____

_____

_____

_____

PRAY

If studying alone, ask the Holy Spirit to reveal the truth about Himself to you. If in a group, take some time to pray for each other as you think about the truths discussed in this session.

EXPLORE

Do you want to go deeper with this teaching? Here are some additional things to think about, pray for, or write about in your journal throughout the next week:

Key Thought

Sin always takes you farther than you wanted to go, costs you more than you wanted to pay, and requires more than you wanted to give.

How would you encourage another believer who is struggling with shame over past sins?

_____

_____

_____

_____

Key Verses
Luke 15:11–13; Genesis 25:29–34; Hebrews 12:1–2; 1 Corinthians 1:18
What truths stand out to you as you read these verses?

_____

_____

What is the Holy Spirit saying to you through these Scriptures?

_____

_____

Key Question
How does God respond when Satan tries to play a trump card against you?

Key Prayer
Heavenly Father, thank You for the cross. Thank You, Jesus, for paying the price for all my secrets, sin, and shame. Holy Spirit, please show me any area of my life that isn't completely surrendered to You. I don't want to give the enemy any trump cards. Help me walk in the light and claim my inheritance as a firstborn child of God. In Jesus' name, Amen.

5

THE FATHER'S BATTLE

God doesn't care where you've been or what you've done. He just wants you to come home.

RECAP

In the previous session, we learned that Satan tries to use the secrets, sin, and shame in our lives as trump cards against us. We need to bring our secrets into the light, and we must deal with sin right away. Shame is a result of the fall, but Jesus paid the price for our freedom. When we bring everything to the cross, we can live in victory.

Did Satan try to use any secrets, sin, or shame against you this past week? If so, how did you respond?

ENGAGE

If you became the world's most brilliant scientist tomorrow, what problem would you solve first?

WATCH

Watch "The Father's Battle."
- Look at how God values us as His children.
- Consider the joy in finding something or someone that was lost.

(If you are not able to watch this teaching on video, read the following. Otherwise, skip to the **Talk** section after viewing.)

READ

Through the parables of the lost sheep, lost coin, and lost son, Luke 15 tells us three important things Jesus wants us to know about ourselves:

You Are Precious

Then all the tax collectors and the sinners drew near to Him to hear Him. And the Pharisees and scribes complained, saying, "This Man receives sinners and eats with them." So He spoke this parable to them, saying:

"What man of you, having a hundred sheep, if he loses one of them, does not leave the ninety-nine in the wilderness, and go after the one which is lost until he finds it? And when he has found *it,* he lays *it* on his shoulders, rejoicing. And when he comes home, he calls together *his* friends and neighbors, saying to them, 'Rejoice with me, for I have found my sheep which was lost!' I say to you that likewise there will be more joy in heaven over one sinner who repents than over ninety-nine just persons who need no repentance (Luke 15:1–7).

The shepherd represents Jesus. In John 10:11, Jesus says clearly, "I am the good shepherd. The good shepherd gives His life for the sheep."

The point of the first parable is **you are precious**. Think about it. The shepherd has 100 sheep. When he loses one, he doesn't stay with the 99; he goes after the missing one. Then the shepherd says,

"I have found my sheep" (v. 6). Jesus knows all His sheep, and every one of us are precious to Him.

Notice also that the shepherd doesn't send someone else to find the missing sheep. Instead, he himself goes. I love that phrase—"He Himself." It's in many places in the Bible, including Hebrews 1:3, 2:18, and 13:5. Jesus Himself laid His life down for us. Prophesying about the Messiah, Isaiah wrote:

> He saw that *there was* no man,
> And wondered that *there was* no intercessor;
> Therefore His own arm brought salvation."

Jesus didn't send someone else to find you. He Himself came to get you.

You Are Valuable

"Or what woman, having ten silver coins, if she loses one coin, does not light a lamp, sweep the house, and search carefully until she finds *it*? And when she has found *it,* she calls *her* friends and neighbors together, saying, 'Rejoice with me, for I have found the piece which I lost!' Likewise, I say to you, there is joy in the presence of the angels of God over one sinner who repents" (Luke 15:8-10).

Jesus uses the example of a coin because He is trying to show value, and in my opinion, He uses a woman to represent the Holy Spirit. Women are often more in touch with their emotions than men are. The Holy Spirit feels joy, and He also grieves for us. James 4:5 says, "Do you think that the Scripture says in vain, 'The Spirit who dwells in us yearns jealously'?" There is a difference between good jealously and bad jealousy. Bad jealousy relates to how something affects you. Good jealousy relates to how something affects another person.

The root word of *silver* in Hebrew means 'desirable.' The woman in the parable had nine coins left, but she *yearned* for the one she lost. The shepherd still had 99 sheep. But he grieved for the stray one.

These silver coins had the image of the ruler on them. Jesus said to give to Caesar what is Caesar's (Matthew 22:21). Whose image is on you? You were created in the image and the likeness of God. The value of anything is determined by what someone's willing to pay for it, and God paid the blood of His Son for you. He paid the same price for you that He paid for any leader you see in the body of Christ. There is no one more valuable to God than you.

You Are Unique

Then He said: "A certain man had two sons. And the younger of them said to *his* father, 'Father, give me the portion of goods that falls *to me.'* So he divided to them *his* livelihood. And not many days after, the younger son gathered all together, journeyed to a far country, and there wasted his possessions with prodigal living. But when he had spent all, there arose a severe famine in that land, and he began to be in want. Then he went and joined himself to a citizen of that country, and he sent him into his fields to feed swine. And he would gladly have filled his stomach with the pods that the swine ate, and no one gave him *anything*.

But when he came to himself, he said, 'How many of my father's hired servants have bread enough and to spare, and I perish with hunger! I will arise and go to my father, and will say to him, "Father, I have sinned against heaven and before you, and I am no longer worthy to be called your son. Make me like one of your hired servants."'

And he arose and came to his father. But when he was still a great way off, his father saw him and had compassion, and ran and fell on his neck and kissed him" (Luke 15:11–20).

I am going to talk about a difficult subject now, and I don't mean to be insensitive toward anyone who has experienced this tragedy. I give this illustration because the Lord used it to show me the fallacy of my thinking. Debbie and I have never had a miscarriage or lost a child, though we do have several grandchildren in heaven. When I heard about couples going through the heartache of losing a child, I used to think, "Well, do they have other children?" Then the Lord showed me that **each** child is unique. If you lose a child, even if you have other children, you still grieve. It still breaks your heart. Why? Because that child is unique. You are unique too. It is easy to believe that God loves us as a group, but God loves you *as a person*.

God created everything: every animal, plant, star, mountain, and ocean. He has the ability and the knowledge to know *you* personally. Nobody has the exact same DNA you have. God designed it. Nobody has the same fingerprints. God designed them while you were in your mother's womb. This is the reason why the father grieved for the prodigal son, even though he had another son at home. He missed his lost son!

There is one major difference in the third parable compared to the first two. Remember, in the first story, the shepherd goes and gets the lost sheep and brings it home. Then the woman looks for and finds the lost coin and puts it back in her collection. But the father doesn't go get the lost son. Why? *Because the son has a choice.*

The father's battle is *waiting*—waiting for his child to come home. If the father had gone and brought his son home, the son's body would have been there, but his heart would still have been lost. We are created in the image of God. Since God has a will, you have a will. The shepherd, the woman, and the father were all looking: The father saw his son when he was "a great way off" (Luke 15:20). He just couldn't go get him and bring him home.

The son is a person, not a sheep or a coin. He has a will. He can decide whether he comes home or not. **God doesn't care where you've been or what you've done. He just wants you to come home.** Jesus died for what you've done and where you've been, and the Holy Spirit is turning the light on so you can see how to get home. The Father is waiting.

NOTES

_____

_____

_____

_____

_____

_____

_____

_____

_____

_____

_____

_____

_____

_____

_____

_____

_____

_____

_____

_____

_____

TALK

These questions can be used for group discussion or personal reflection.

Question 1

Have you ever lost something extremely valuable and then found it? How did you feel? How do you think God feels when His lost children return home?

_____

_____

_____

_____

Question 2

Read Hebrews 1:3, 2:18, and 13:5. How does it make you feel to know that Jesus Himself came to save you from sin?

_____

_____

_____

_____

Question 3

In what ways are believers similar to the woman's lost coin?

_____

_____

_____

_____

Question 4

Read Luke 15. How is the parable of the lost son different than the other two parables?

_____

_____

_____

_____

PRAY

If studying alone, ask the Holy Spirit to reveal the truth about Himself to you. If in a group, take some time to pray for each other as you think about the truths discussed in this session.

EXPLORE

Do you want to go deeper with this teaching? Here are some additional things to think about, pray for, or write about in your journal throughout the next week:

Key Thought

The value of anything is determined by what someone is willing to pay for it. And God paid the blood of His Son for you.

Do you ever see yourself as more or less valuable than other believers? How do you think God sees you?

_____

_____

_____

_____

Key Verses
Luke 5:1–24; John 10:11; Hebrews 13:5; James 4:5

What truths stand out to you as you read these verses?

_____

_____

What is the Holy Spirit saying to you through these Scriptures?

_____

_____

Key Question
Is there any area of your life in which God is waiting for you to come home?

Key Prayer
Lord, thank You for making a way for me to come home when I was hopelessly lost. I was buried beneath the weight of my sin, but You picked me up and gave me new life. I am so grateful to be Your child! Help me remember how much You love me, even when I make mistakes. You are a wonderful Father, and I submit to Your will. In Jesus' name, Amen.

6

THE EVERYDAY BATTLE

God wants to have two-way, intentional communication with us every day.

RECAP

In the previous session, we learned that every person is precious, valuable, and unique to God. He made you in His image, and He knows every single detail about your life. No matter what you've done or how badly you've messed up, God is waiting for you How has knowing how special you are to God affected your relationship with Him?

ENGAGE

If you had to choose one meal to eat every day for the rest of your life, what would it be and why?

WATCH

Watch "The Everyday Battle."
- Look for the difference between talking *to* someone and talking *with* someone.
- Consider how you can use these guidelines to improve your quiet time.

(If you are not able to watch this teaching on video, read the following. Otherwise, skip to the **Talk** section after viewing.)

READ

The everyday battle is the easiest battle to win. The only way you lose this battle is by not showing up.

In Luke 15:30, the older brother complains about the warm reception his prodigal brother received. Here is the father's response in verse 31: "Son, you are always with me, and all that I have is yours." Think about God saying that to you: *I'm always with you.*

We already know that the older son had an attitude problem, but why? I believe it is because he failed the everyday battle. He was living in the house with his father, but I'm not sure he was *communing* with his father. In other words, the older brother was there physically but not emotionally or spiritually.

In Exodus 25:22, speaking about the tabernacle, God says, "And there I will **meet with** you, and I will **speak with** you" (emphasis added). Here is the everyday battle: Are you really meeting with God every day, and are you speaking *with* God every day? Or are you just talking *to* Him? It really does make a difference.

Many of us think of meeting with God as having "quiet time." Back in the 80s, there were manuals about how to have a quiet time. I think they should have been titled, "How to Have a Busy Time." I can remember getting one of these and having to pray for so many people every day and reading so many Scriptures every day. This was supposed to relieve my stress, but it didn't work. I got behind in both my prayers and my reading, and the more behind I was, the more stressed I was. I certainly wasn't having "time with God."

I believe in praying and reading your Bible every day. But I want to ask you a question: Are you meeting *with* a person each day, or are you going through a regimen of what you're supposed to pray about today and how many Scriptures you're supposed to read? The older brother was in the house, but he wasn't really communicating with his father. How many believers in the body of Christ are not really communicating with their heavenly Father?

Think of it like a marriage. If you only spend as much time with your spouse as you do with God, or if you are only as open with your spouse as you are with God, would you have marriage problems?

Before I talk about how to have a quiet time, I want to address some common misconceptions many people have.

Four Myths About Quiet Times

1. Your quiet time must be between 4:00 a.m. and 6:00 a.m.

This is *not* in the Bible. I tried this and fell asleep on God. He said, "Go back to bed. You're incoherent at this time!" I asked Him if He'd be open later.

If you're an early riser, that's okay. I believe you should schedule your quiet time, and, like tithing, it should be the *first* of your day. But some of us need to get coffee first.

2. Your quiet time must last at least an hour.

There's nothing in the Bible about this either. You've probably heard of people who pray three or four hours each day. Those people are either unemployed or don't have children. There is no prescribed amount of time for quiet time.

3. **Your quiet time journal must sound like the Bible.**

Pastor Olen is one of our apostolic elders and my former pastor at Shady Grove Church. He read some of his journal at an elders' meeting, and it was like hearing *My Utmost for His Highest*. I thought it sounded phenomenal, and I wondered what my entry for that day said. Here's what I had written: "Try not to be a jerk today."

4. **Your quiet time must be every day.**

I think you should pray and read your Bible every day, but what happens if you have an early flight or something happened the night before? If you miss a few days or even weeks, you feel bad about going back. What's God going to say? We think He's going to chew us out, so we just don't go. However, God's not going to do that. Why? Because it's a relationship.

Years ago, the Lord gave me four guidelines about having a quiet time. They may not be exactly the same for you, but hopefully these will help.

Four Guidelines for Quiet Time

1. **Quiet Your Mind**

The battle is in our minds. When you try to spend time with God, your mind often interrupts your thoughts with things of this world. You need to remove your busy thoughts that distract you from the Lord. It usually takes me anywhere from three to ten minutes to quiet my mind. Sometimes I even put my fingers in my ears, odd as it sounds.

In Psalm 62:1, David writes, "Truly my soul silently *waits* for God." Verse 5 says, "My soul, wait silently for God alone." Wait silently.

2. Focus Your Mind

When I asked the Lord about the second step I should do, He said, "Sing." I asked, "Have you heard me sing?" He said, "Yes, and I love it."

Many years ago, I was in a start-up church where the worship team was terrible. I asked the Lord if He heard it, and He said, "Yes, it sounds great, doesn't it?" The music itself wasn't great, but God reminded me of the verse that says He looks at the heart of man. Well, God not only *looks* at the heart, but He also *listens* to the heart. He told me, "I've heard people who had terrible voices, but their hearts were great, and it sounds beautiful. I've heard others who had great voices but bad hearts, and it's horrible."

I asked the Lord what song He wanted me to sing, and He said, "The one you wake up with." How often have you awakened with a song on your mind? God gives us a song every morning that is the key into the Holy of Holies.

Psalm 100:2 says, "Come before His presence with singing." It doesn't matter what you sing. Just think of a worship song and sing it in your mind to God. This is how you enter God's presence.

3. Pray Your Mind

This is simple. Just pray what is on your mind. This is not inter-cessory prayer, where you pray about many things for other people. This is your quiet time. You don't have to pray for world peace if it's not on your mind. Pray for your family; pray for whatever is going on that day. Talk to God about those things that burden you.

First Peter 5:7 says, "Casting all your care upon Him, for He cares for you." Do this every morning and you will be shocked how it will change your day. The word *casting* means 'to throw.' Throw it on God. You were not designed to *carry*—you were designed to *cast*. You are a sheep, and sheep do not carry burdens. The shepherd carries the burdens.

Many times we say that we laid something at God's feet, but then we take it back. Prayer is the *transference of* a burden. If you come out of your prayer closet and you're still burdened, you didn't pray—you just griped.

4. Renew Your Mind

We renew our minds with God's Word. Just read somewhere in the Bible and use a version you can understand. Often what I read in the morning is exactly what I need for that day.

The Lord convicted me one summer of having "drive-through" quiet times. He said, "I want you to come in and have a meal with Me." A few weeks later, I went upstairs to have my quiet time. An hour and a half later, I came back downstairs, but I had no idea it had been that long. Quiet times aren't boring when you're actually spending time with God. But when you're trying to go through a list or fulfill a duty, it's hard. I've had times like that, too. For example, I've made commitments such as "I'm going to pray 30 minutes a day." Then I pray everything I can think of, look at my watch, and think, *Only seven minutes? Twenty-three more minutes ...*

That's not what God wants. He just wants to talk to His kids. If I could help you in any way, I'd convince you to make a commitment to spend some time with God every day, at least as often as you can. Can you imagine how it would change your life?

NOTES

_____

_____

_____

_____

_____

_____

_____

_____

_____

_____

_____

TALK

These questions can be used for group discussion or personal reflection.

Question 1

Why do you think some people dislike the phrase "quiet time"? What are some challenges you have faced when you try to meet with God?

_____

_____

_____

_____

Question 2

How do you think God would respond if you missed your quiet time tomorrow? Would He be angry? Why or why not?

_____

_____

_____

_____

Question 3

Read Psalm 62:1, 5. Why is it important to quiet your mind when you meet with God?

_____

_____

_____

_____

Question 4

Why do you think the Bible tell us to "cast our burdens" on God? Why can't we carry them ourselves?

_____

_____

_____

_____

Question 5

List two or three ways that meeting with God could change your life.

_____

_____

_____

_____

PRAY

If studying alone, ask the Holy Spirit to reveal the truth about Himself to you. If in a group, take some time to pray for each other as you think about the truths discussed in this session.

EXPLORE

Do you want to go deeper with this teaching? Here are some additional things to think about, pray for, or write about in your journal throughout the next week:

Key Thought

Are you meeting with a person each day, or are you through a regimen of what you're supposed to pray about today and how many Scriptures you're supposed to read?

How would you encourage someone who has experienced difficulties with their quiet times?

_____

_____

_____

_____

Key Verses

Luke 15:31; Psalm 62:1; 100:2; 1 Peter 5:7

What truths stand out to you as you read these verses?

_____

_____

What is the Holy Spirit saying to you through these Scriptures?

_____

_____

Key Question

What changes do you need to make to your daily routine in order to meet with God regularly?

Key Prayer

Heavenly Father, thank You for the privilege of spending time with You. Please forgive me for putting any person or thing ahead of You. You are the most important Person in my life, and I want to get to know You better every day. Help me quiet my mind and hear Your voice as I spend time in Your presence. I love You. In Jesus' name, Amen.

LEADER'S GUIDE

The *Lost and Found* Leader's Guide is designed to help you lead your small group or class through the *Lost and Found* curriculum. Use this guide along with the curriculum for a life-changing, interactive experience.

BEFORE YOU MEET

- Ask God to prepare the hearts and minds of the people in your group. Ask Him to show you how to encourage each person to integrate the principles all of you discover into your daily lives through group discussion and writing in your journals.
- Preview the video segment for the week.
- Plan how much time you'll give to each portion of your meeting (see the suggested schedule below). In case you're unable to get through all of the activities in the time you have planned, here is a list of the most important questions (from the **Talk** section) for each week.

SUGGESTED SCHEDULE FOR THE GROUP:

- **Engage** and **Recap** (5 Minutes)
- **Watch** and **Read** (20 Minutes)
- **Talk** (25 Minutes)
- **Pray** (10 minutes)

SESSION ONE

Q: Read Hebrews 10:39 and James 1:21. What is the difference between the finished work of grace in your spirit and the progressive work of grace in your soul?

Q: Why is feeding your spirit with the Word of God essential to winning the battle with your soul?

SESSION TWO

Q: How does Scripture define *integrity?* How does this definition contrast with the world's view of "honesty"?

Q: Read Acts 5:1–3. Why do you think integrity is so important to God?

SESSION THREE

Q: Why did Jesus tell the parables in Luke 15? What is the emphasis of these three stories?

Q: Why did the prodigal son miss out on his father's presence and provision? Why did the older brother miss out on the same things?

SESSION FOUR

Q: What are the three common trump cards the enemy tries to use against believers?

Q: Why is it important to deal with "little" sins before they grow?

SESSION FIVE

Q: Have you ever lost something extremely valuable and then found it? How did you feel? How do you think God feels when His lost children return home?

Q: Read Luke 15. How is the parable of the lost son different than the other two parables?

SESSION SIX

Q: Why do you think some people dislike the phrase "quiet time"? What are some challenges you have faced when you try to meet with God?

Q: Why do you think the Bible tell us to "cast our burdens" on God? Why can't we carry them ourselves?

HOW TO USE THE CURRICULUM

This study has a simple design.

The One Thing

This is a brief statement under each session title that sums up the main point—the key idea—of the session.

Recap
Recap the previous week's session, inviting members to share about any opportunities they have encountered throughout the week that apply what they learned (this doesn't apply to the first week).

Engage
Ask the icebreaker question to help get people talking and feeling comfortable with one another.

Watch
Watch the videos (recommended).

Read
If you're unable to watch the videos, read these sections.

Talk
The questions in these lessons are intentionally open-ended. Use them to help the group members reflect on Scripture and the lesson.

Pray
Ask members to share their concerns and then pray together. Be sensitive to the Holy Spirit and the needs of the group.

Explore
Encourage members to complete the written portion in their books before the next meeting.

KEY TIPS FOR THE LEADER

- Generate participation and discussion.
- Resist the urge to teach. The goal is for great conversation that leads to discovery.
- Ask open-ended questions—questions that can't be answered with "yes" or "no" (e.g., "What do you think about that?" rather than "Do you agree?").
- When a question arises, ask the group for their input instead of answering it yourself before allowing anyone else to respond.
- Be comfortable with silence. If you ask a question and no one responds, rephrase the question and wait for a response. Your primary role is to create an environment where people feel comfortable to be themselves and participate, not to provide the answers to all of their questions.
- Ask the group to pray for each other from week to week, especially about key issues that arise during your group time. This is how you begin to build authentic community and encourage spiritual growth within the group.

KEYS TO A DYNAMIC SMALL GROUP

Relationships

Meaningful, encouraging relationships are the foundation of a dynamic small group. Teaching, discussion, worship, and prayer are important elements of a group meeting, but the depth of each element is often dependent upon the depth of the relationships among members.

Availability
Building a sense of community within your group requires members to prioritize their relationships with one another. This means being available to listen, care for one another, and meet each other's needs.

Mutual Respect
Mutual respect is shown when members value each other's opinions (even when they disagree) and are careful never to put down or embarrass others in the group (including their spouses, who may or may not be present).

Openness
A healthy small group environment encourages sincerity and transparency. Members treat each other with grace in areas of weakness, allowing each other room to grow.

Confidentiality
To develop authenticity and a sense of safety within the group, each member must be able to trust that things discussed within the group will not be shared outside the group.

Shared Responsibility

Group members will share the responsibility of group meetings by using their God-given abilities to serve at each gathering. Some may greet, some may host, some may teach, etc. Ideally, each person should be available to care for others as needed.

Sensitivity

Dynamic small groups are born when the leader consistently seeks and is responsive to the guidance of the Holy Spirit, following His leading throughout the meeting as opposed to sticking to the "agenda." This guidance is especially important during the discussion and ministry time.

Fun!

Dynamic small groups take the time to have fun! Create an atmosphere for fun and be willing to laugh at yourself every now and then!

ABOUT THE AUTHOR

Robert Morris is the lead senior pastor of Gateway Church, a multicampus church in the Dallas/ Fort Worth Metroplex. Since it began in 2000, the church has grown to more than 39,000 active members. His television program is aired in over 190 countries, and his radio feature, *Worship & the Word with Pastor Robert,* airs on radio stations across America. He serves as chancellor of The King's University and is the bestselling author of 15 books including *The Blessed Life, Truly Free, Frequency*, and *Beyond Blessed*. Robert and his wife, Debbie, have been married 38 years and are blessed with one married daughter, two married sons, and nine grandchildren. He lives in Dallas, TX.

More resources for your small group by Pastor Robert Morris!

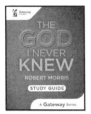

Study Guide: 978-1-945529-54-2
DVD: 978-1-949399-41-7

Study Guide: 978-1-949399-54-7
DVD: 978-1-949399-51-6

Study Guide: 978-1-945529-51-1
DVD: 978-1-949399-49-3

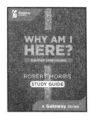

Study Guide: 978-1-945529-71-9
DVD: 978-1-949399-50-9

DVD + Discussion Guide:
978-1-949399-68-4

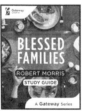

Study Guide: 978-1-949399-55-4
DVD: 978-1-949399-52-3

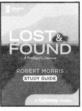

Study Guide: 978-1-945529-85-6
DVD: 978-1-949399-48-6

Study Guide: 978-1-945529-56-6
DVD: 978-1-949399-43-1

Study Guide: 978-1-945529-55-9
DVD: 978-1-949399-42-4

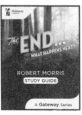

Study Guide: 978-1-945529-88-7
DVD: 978-1-949399-53-0

Study Guide: 978-1-949399-65-3
DVD: 978-1-949399-66-0

Study Guide: 978-0-997429-84-8
DVD: 978-1-949399-46-2

You can find these resources and others at
www.gatewaypublishing.com

NOTES